Listen T
Give Y
Positive Attention And Enjoy Those Daily Moments.

Jennifer N. Smith

Copyright © 2016 Jennifer N. Smith
All rights reserved.

ISBN: 1535063033

ISBN-13: 978-1535063036

CONTENTS

1	Introduction	1
2	Are You Expecting Too Much from Your Children	5
3	Begging for Attention	10
4	Start Making Changes Today	14
5	Changing The Way We Look at Parenting	18
6	Time to Slow Down	22
7	Conclusion	26

Introduction

You climb out of bed each morning with an entire list of things to do on your mind. It does not matter if you are a stay at home mom, a working mom or a single parent, we all have loads of things to get done.

It generally starts with getting the kids ready for school, making breakfast, brushing hair and making sure everyone has everything they need for the day. If you have smaller children, this time of the day can be even more hectic.

The kids are talking, trying to tell you about their dream, what they are going to do at school that day or just trying to make conversation with you but you are too busy to deal with that. You have to check your email, your phone ......

Mom, Spend Time With Me Please!

After the older children are off, you may have to drop the younger ones off at daycare or you may have time to pick up your house a bit. If you have little ones following you around this can be difficult because they want to play, they want to spend time with you and the truth is, there just is not time for it.

Then it is off to work where you might get to relax for a few moments during the day before coming back home and dealing with even more chaos.

The afternoon rush is difficult for us all. There is homework, kids wanting to talk about their day, chores to do, dinner to cook and bills to pay. On top of all of this we have phone calls to return, emails to answer, baths to give and dishes to do.

"Stop Yelling And Love Me More, Please Mom!"
Positive Parenting Is Easier Than You Think

Our lives are hectic. Many people have simply accepted this as the norm today, **but have you ever sat down after a long day,** your kids are in bed and you don't even feel like you got to spend one moment with them. **Guilt begins to fill you as you wonder what it was that they were trying to tell you that morning or what is actually going on at school.**

Now imagine how your children feel. Did you ever feel like there was someone in your life that was just too busy for you? Think about how it saddened you to feel that you were not important enough to that person for them to make time for you. When your children go to bed at night, **they know that the person in their life that is too busy for them is their parent.**

Children do not understand, no matter how much we want them to, that chores have to be done and bills have to be paid. They do not understand why you have time to talk on the phone but not to them. **This has to stop.** We are raising a generation that does not know what it is like to interact with their parents. We are raising a generation that is in essence raising themselves. We are just keeping them alive.

It is time to put down the phone, slow down, stop taking on so much and spend time with our children. We are their examples and if we do not interact with them, not only are they going to have very low self-esteem because they will not feel that they are worth our time but they will not know how to interact with those around them.

Chapter 1- Are You Expecting Too Much from Your Children

It is so easy to become so busy today that we expect our children to pick up our slack, but are we as parents expecting too much from our children. I am not talking about having a child do specific chores or helping around the house, although that is one thing that does happen. What I am talking about is that we are expecting our children to know how to survive without us.

Of course we are present. We are occupying the same space as the child. We provide a home for them, food to eat, and clothes to wear, but are we really present in their lives?

Think about the last time your child told you something was going on at school be it good or bad. If the experience was good, they were excited to share it with you. They were proud of something they had accomplished or they enjoyed the experience and wanted you to know about it, they wanted you to be proud of them. If on the other hand, the experience was bad, they needed you to be there for them. They needed someone to tell them that it would be okay and to show them that they were important.

Did you give your child what they were looking for or did you just blow them off, not really paying attention to what they said?

How can you know if you have done this? How can you tell if you have not paid enough attention to what your child has to say or that you have made them feel unimportant?

There are a few ways, the first way is that you will feel it. You will feel a disconnect with your child and that you will know you have been too busy. That is probably what led you to read this book, **but how do you know that it has affected your child?**

1. Your child will no longer share their fears with you. They may no longer tell you about their failures either. If you find that your child is hiding their failures from you, it is likely that they do not feel secure in telling you about them. This could happen for several reasons, one of them is that you overreact, but it could also happen because the child does not feel like you will listen to them. You are supposed to be your child's safe place. You are the one person that they should be able to go to and talk about anything including their fears and failures. If you do not put value on what they have to say, chances are, they are going to stop coming to you with these types of conversations.

2. Your child could lose interest in the things that he or she once loved. Often times, if a parent does not show interest in what a child loves, they will lose interest in it as well. Of course, if you put too much pressure on a child to take part in a specific activity, they can lose interest in it too. Imagine that your child loves baseball, but you don't have time to play, you don't have time to go to practice and when you are at the games, you are on your cell phone. Your child will pick up on this and they will quickly lose interest in what they are doing because they sense that you are not proud of what they are doing. It has no value to you so it loses the value it once had with them.

3. **If you find that you are more concerned with the outcome than the process,** you may not be giving your child the amount of attention they need. Think about this: It is time to build a valentines day box, you purchase all of the supplies and instead of having fun, playing and making a mess with your child while they build the box, you just put it together because you don't want a mess and you want to be proud of the box they take to school. You have taken all of the joy out of making the box, all of the creativity is gone for the child and they didn't get to spend time with you because you cared more about the outcome than the process of making the box

4. **You do nothing that is enjoyable with your children.** It is so easy to become so busy that you just don't have time to take a day off. You work during the week and have a home to take care of, bills to pay and shopping to do on the weekend. When do you spend time with your children? Most of us simply don't. There are no more weekend outings, but we have to make time for these. This is when memories are made and when you as a parent can relax and just enjoy your family.

5. **Finally, if the sound of your child speaking has simply become part of the background noise in your life, it may be time to start listening to what they have to say.** We have all been there at some point, we just zone out and don't really hear what is being said, but if this is happening more often than not, it is time to take a step back and figure out what is really important to you.

Expecting our children to accept that we are simply too busy for them because they will understand 'someday' is no longer acceptable.

We are raising the next generation and if we as their parents do not step up and pay attention to them, really listen to what is being said, we are crippling the next generation!

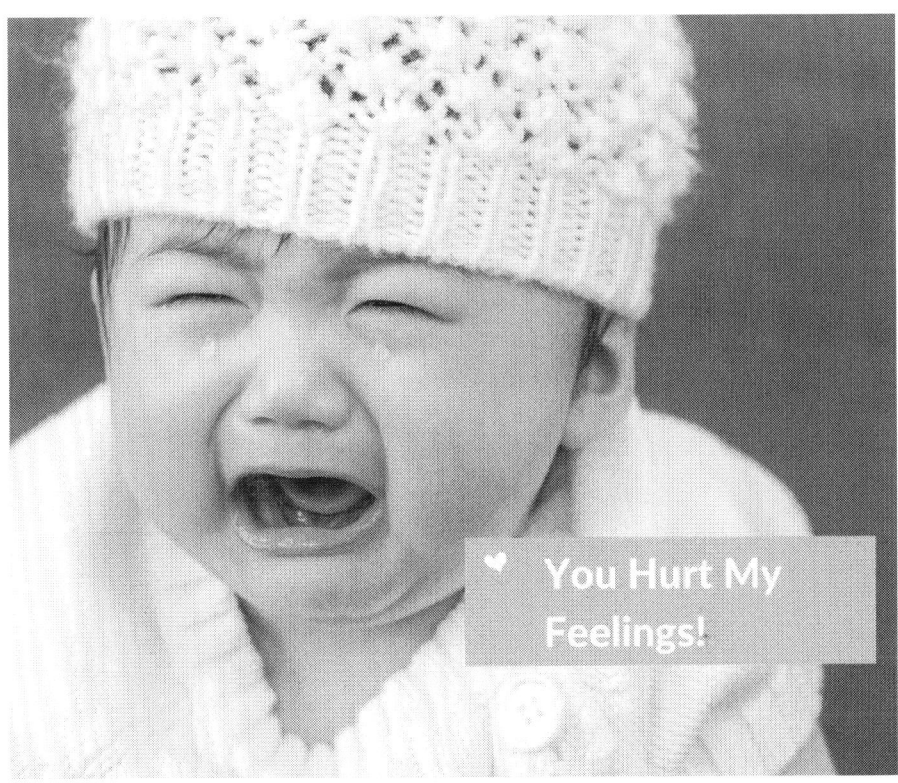

Chapter 2- Begging for Attention

One of the biggest signs that a parent has become too busy and is not giving their child the attention that they need is **bad behavior.** I am not saying that all bad behavior stems from lack of attention because there are specific disorders that can cause a child to have outbursts as well, but this is one of the first things that should be looked at when a child is displaying bad behavior.

You see, the fact is that to a child, any attention is better than no attention at all. So they would rather have your attention, even if it is negative than to feel as if you do not know they are there. This type of behavior can be as simple as a child trying to be the center of attention when you have company over, trying to interrupt conversations, trying to talk to you while you are on the

phone, acting out in public or having problems with behavior at school.

Many times, this type of behavior is displayed because the child has no idea how to get you to pay attention to them if they are not misbehaving. Of course, this is not their fault, it is natural for them to want the attention of their parents. It is our job as parents to **show them the difference between good and bad attention as well as how to get the good attention.**

Many parents with children that misbehave have found that ignoring that behavior while praising the good behavior reinforces the good behavior and the child will learn that they will not get a reaction out of you when they are misbehaving. On the other hand, when you are too busy to reinforce good behavior, you are paying attention to the bad behavior, giving the child the attention they are seeking and therefore teaching them **that is the appropriate way for them to get your attention.**

When a child misbehaves as a means to get the attention they desire, it is often because they lack self-confidence. They feel that there is no place for them if they are not the center of attention, the attention that the child is receiving makes them feel that they matter.

There is also another type of behavior that is displayed when a child is not getting the attention they need. The first child is more outspoken than the second type of child we will talk about. The second type of child is quiet, shy and uses their charm to get people to do the things that they want them to do. When they cannot get people to do what they want or get what they need from people they begin to pout or they withdraw from those around them. Many people think that this is a sign of an underlying problem but it is not. This is just the way this type of child manipulates those around them to get the attention they desire.

Imagine a world where you try to interact with people and they do not acknowledge that you are even there. That is the type of world that your child is living in. We all have to have people that we can interact with every day. We need people that we can talk to and that will allow us to express ourselves. **You are that person for your child.**

If you want your child's behavior to change, you are going to have to make a change as well. Instead of paying attention to them when they are misbehaving, pay attention to them when they are behaving well, **when they have accomplished something or when they feel proud of themselves.**

This is not to say that you should not discipline a child when they misbehave. You should teach your child not to misbehave, but you need to do so in a manner that does not provide them with the attention they are seeking. Provide them with that attention when they are behaving well instead.

Chapter 3- Start Making Changes Today

The good news is that this book is going to help you start making the changes that you need to make to ensure your child is getting the attention that they need. No matter how long you have allowed life to keep you too busy to give your children the attention that they need, no matter how you feel right now, even if you think that there is no way for you to change this, you are going to be able to make the changes you need to make with the information in this book.

The good news is that you <u>do not</u> have to drop everything and focus on your children every waking minute of every day. Spending some time with them each day, letting them know that they matter to you.

START MAKING CHANGES TODAY

SPEND TIME TOGETHER

There are many different ways for you to make ways for you to make time for your children and I want to go over a few things that you can do in this chapter.

1. **Limit the amount of time that you are spending online.** This may seem a little odd considering this book is available online, but think about the number of hours you spend on social media, checking your email or just playing games. The majority of people are spending at least one hour online each day, **imagine what a difference it would make if you just spent half of that time with your child.**

2. **Limit the amount of time that you spend watching television**. It is okay for you to watch your favorite television show once a week, but there is no need to sit down and have a nightly Movie binge. Instead, go outside and play with your kids or help

them clean their bedrooms. Remember, no matter what it is that you are doing with your children, they are going to appreciate it.

3. **Get your children involved in what you are doing.** If you are working in the yard, get the kids involved, if you are doing dishes, have them help you rinse and dry them. These are great ways for you to spend time with your children while getting the things done that you need to get done. This will allow your children to talk to you about what is going on in their lives and they will know how important to you they are.

4. **Make dinners, special.** Even if you are just having leftovers, make sure that you are eating at the table, light a few candles and turn on some relaxing music. Dinner is a great time for you to talk to your children about how their day went. Stop thinking about work, stop thinking about the bills that you need to pay and how much you need to get done. Focus on your children and just enjoy the time that you have with them.

5. **Spend time reading together each night.** Even if you are just reading a short book, or if you are having your child read a book to you, your children are going to love spending this time with you. It is going to make them feel like they are important to you and it is going to help them with their reading skills.

The truth is, parents are busier now than parents of generations past. It may feel like the world is moving faster or that there are less hours in a day, but the truth is, we as parents have begun taking on more and more expecting that we can handle it all. The problem is that our children are the ones that are suffering.

Another issue is that more mothers are in the workplace than ever before. I am not saying this to make anyone feel badly. The majority of homes need two incomes in order to make it work and there is no getting around that, but what you can do is focus on using the time that you do have at home to communicate with your children.

Many parents do not understand where their time is going, they get lost in their day and do not get all of the things done that they need to get done, this makes them feel as if there is no time left to spend with their children.

If you are struggling to figure out where your time is going, **try keeping a time journal**. Write down what you are doing during the day. Track the time you are at work, track the time you spend online, the time that you spend doing chores at home and the time that you spend in front of the television. This will help you find the time that you are looking for to spend time with your children.

It is time for you to start deciding what your priorities are in life. You also have to remember that your children are only going to be young for a short period of time. Before you know it, they will be moving out and starting a life of their own. Do you want them to live the same type of life that you are living now or do you want them to know how to balance their lives and find time to spend with their own children? **Be the example that you want your children to follow when they grow up.**

Chapter 4- Changing The Way We Look at Parenting

When we have children, something changes inside of us. We want to give our children everything we never had. We want to provide them with a big house, a nice yard to play in, a room full of toys and comfortable furniture, **but we often forget that none of that stuff matters to kids.**

Of course, children are going to be children and they are going to tell you that they want the latest toys, the best of everything. **The truth is, they would much rather have time with you**. One of the reasons that many parents are purchasing all types of new toys and new electronics is because they feel guilty for not spending time with their children. This is why we are raising a generation of spoiled and entitled children that do not respect the things that are purchased for them. They know that they can guilt mom and dad into buying them new stuff if they break what they have.

Parenting is not simply keeping a child alive until they move out of your house, it is about teaching them how to be a productive adult. Being a parent means that you are in charge of supporting your child not just financially, but emotionally, socially, physically and intellectually as well.

This also does not end when the child moves out of the house.

One huge mistake that many parents make is that they put their needs before the needs of their children. The day that you decided to have a child was the day that you decided to put your child's needs before your own.

When it comes to giving them enough attention, the same thing is true. You are going to have to, as a parent, give up things that you enjoy or that are important to you in order to give your child the attention that he or she needs.

Many people have been led to believe that they should not have to give up the things that they love just because they are parents and I believe this is where a huge mistake was made. After years of being told that parents don't have to give up the things they love in order to be good parents, many have begun to believe this and it simply is not true. You do have to decide what it is that you love the most. Are your children more important to you or are your hobbies more important to you? Are your children what matters in your life or is it social media?

We as parents need to take a step back and ask ourselves what we really want out of life. Do we want a huge bank account with children that never come and see us when they grow up or do we want children that are well adjusted and know how much we care about them?

It is important that you understand, no one is trying to make you feel guilty but simply give you a reality check. The truth is that no matter how much you want to; you simply cannot do it all. **The idea of being a super mom has made many of us think that we should be able to but it is not possible.**

We need to remind ourselves that we cannot give 100 percent of ourselves to everything that we do and for that reason we need to take a few moments and look at what we are doing with our time. **We need to get our priorities straight.**

Finally, I think that it is important for you to remember that you are the adult. You are responsible for the life of your child, you are responsible for ensuring they are capable of being productive, well-adjusted adults when they grow up. Far too many parents are taking time away from their children so that they can go out and try to experience the 'fun' that they feel they missed out on. This can lead to children feeling that they do not matter to their parents. The parents can also push off too much responsibility onto the children. Simply taking the time and looking at your life will help you find the time that you are lacking with your child.

Sit down and think about what type of parent you want to be. Create a plan so that you can be that parent and understand that it is not going to happen overnight. When you make changes in your life, you have to make them slowly and accept that there will be times when you will fail.

Chapter 5- Time to Slow Down

Learning how to slow down is one of the best things that you can do for your children. **One of the best things that you can remember is that the best time for you to spend time with your child is when you don't have time for it.**

Think about that for a moment. The truth is, you should never allow yourself to become so busy that you do not have time for your child. Of course, there are going to be times when you are busier than normal. There are times when I just can't go outside and play because my work load simply does not allow it, but it is during those times that I make sure to make time to sit down for dinner with

the kids and making sure that we have time to talk about their day.

Of course, this is much easier when you have older children because you can explain to them why you do not have extra time on a specific day and it is important for you to do this. It is also important for you to spend extra time with your children later on when you are not as busy.

One great thing that you can do is to make sure that at least one day on the weekend is free to spend with your children. This will ensure that even if you are very busy during the week and only have a little bit of time to spend with them each day, they will know they are the center of your attention for the entire day at least once per week.

For us, that day is Sunday. The entire day belongs to the children and we spend it however they want of course within reason. Each Saturday evening, after all of the chores are done, shopping is taken care of and the bills are paid, before the kids go to bed, we sit down and talk about how we are going to spend our day together.

Learning how to slow down is very important for you as well as for your children. If you find that you are not able to spend time with your children because they have a full schedule, you may decide to clear out their schedule a bit.

When you cut back on what you are doing each day, you will find that you are more relaxed, you are able to be present in the moment and you are able to enjoy it more.

You will have to learn how to slow down without coming to a complete stop. This is something that many people find difficult. If they are not going full force, they are not going at all. Instead, learn how to go at a steady pace, filling your day with things that you need to get done while setting time aside each evening for your family.

One way that you can ensure that you are not taking on too much is to create a daily schedule. This is also a really good way for you to begin to understand just how much time is going to waste each day. Begin by creating a list of all of the things you need to get done, then create a list of things you want to get done. The next thing you should do is to create a daily schedule. Fill in the schedule with all of the things that you need to get done. Once you have done this, fill in the things that you want to get done (if there is time) not forgetting spending time with your children.

Many times, when people do this, they find that they do in fact have much more time than they thought they did.

The truth is that if you create a schedule and stick to it, you will find that you have a few hours free each day and you are not as busy as you thought you were.

Conclusion

When parents do not have enough time to spend with their children, the children will suffer. Children will display bad behavior, they will beg for attention from their parents, they rebel and they withdraw. These children lack the self-confidence and self-esteem that they need and they lack the ability to communicate with those around them.

The good news is that all of this can be turned around and it does not take a lot of work. In fact, by simply slowing down, clearing the clutter out of your life, and making time to spend with your child. By following the tips that you have found in this book, you will be able to ensure that your children are getting the attention that they need in order to be well rounded individuals.

By not focusing on bad behavior and instead giving your child the attention they need, putting the phone down, getting off of the computer or out from in front of the television, you will see your child's behavior turn around quickly. You will find that you are able to relax more and that your child is happier and well adjusted. You will also find that when you go to bed at night, **you no longer have to deal with the guilt you have been dealing with. You will know that you are being the best parent that you can be.**

If you yell at your child, I highly recommend that you read my new book:

Stop Yelling And Love Me More, Please Mom. Positive Parenting Is Easier Than You Think.

We can not raise a happy child if we are constantly screaming threats at them. No parent sets out to hurt their child, but this type of parenting does just that.
To raise a happy child that wants to behave, you need to retrain yourself first. You need to change the way you think and react to their behavior. You need to understand your triggers and heal yourself. Only then you can begin to heal your relationship with your children.

For Self-Improvement Tips and Advice:

Check out my website here:
http://improve-yourself-today.com/

Thank you for reading!

Dear Reader:

I really hope you find it helpful. Finally, I need to ask a favor, as an author, I love feedback. Can you kindly leave a review for this book; Loved it or hated it! Just Let me know.

Thanks in advance

Jennifer N. Smith

Copyright and Disclaimer

All rights reserved. Without limiting the rights under copyright reserved above, no part of this publication maybe reproduced, stored in or introduced into a retrieval system, or transmitted in any form, or by any means (electronic, mechanical, photocopying, recording or otherwise) without the prior written permission of both the copyright owner and the publisher of this book.

ABOUT THE AUTHOR

For me, the hardest part of being a mom is learning how to manage my own emotions. After having a baby, I found myself yelling at my husband and my son every day, I felt horrible and guilty afterward, and I felt so stressed and tired all the time.

I started reading lots of self-help books and I have learned a lot. Now, I feel happier, positive and relaxed and I stopped yelling.

I want to share what I have learned throughout the years with my readers; I hope my books can help you deal with your day-to-day challenges, and make you feel happy again, you can create a home full of peace and love for the whole family.

Motivational Quotes:
http://improve-yourself-today.com/motivational-quotes-page/

Made in the USA
Columbia, SC
28 June 2019